SWANSEA

Thank you for the days!

SWANSEA

Thank you for the days!

by David Roberts

South Wales Evening Post

BRYNGOLD
BOOKS

First published in Great Britain in 2005 by
Bryngold Books Ltd.,
Golden Oaks, 98 Brynau Wood, Cimla,
Neath, South Wales, SA11 3YQ.
www.bryngoldbooks.com

Typesetting, layout and design
by Bryngold Books

ISBN 0-9547859-4-0

Printed in Wales by
Dinefwr Press, Rawlings Road,
Llandybie, Carmarthenshire, SA18 3YD

Contents

An appreciation

Swansea - Thank you for the days would not have been made possible without the valued assistance of readers of the South Wales Evening Post and the many residents of Swansea, past and present, who so willingly submitted their own cherished personal images of days gone by. However small their contribution it is just as valuable in making this a book that is by the people, for the people.
Particular thanks for their assistance are due to:
Cheryl Roberts,
Colin Andrews, Les Saunders, Steve Phillips,
Roy Kneath, Pam Taylor, Clive Cockings,
Terry and Jill Quick, Jean Evans,
Duncan Atkinson, Marylin Evans, Gloria Rees,
Roger Trollope, Sheila Seaward, Alan Giffard,
A Hughes, William Bateman, Hazel Rees,
Clive Williams, David and Gay Mitchell,
E.J Trick, David Beynon, Gerald Gabb,
Huw Evans and Anthony Isaac.
Thanks also to Emyr Nicholas and the
staff at Dinefwr Press

For details of how you can contribute to the next book and in doing so play
a part in this valuable, growing pictorial archive telephone 01639 643961.
All contributions for the next publication will be welcomed and returned after use.

Foreword

SOME people think books of old photographs are nothing more than exercises in nostalgia. There's nothing wrong with being nostalgic, of course, but in fact those people are wrong. The past, especially the past as viewed through the lenses of long departed photographers, can tell us something about who and how we are today.

For example, take a look at the two photographs on page 21 of this, the latest in David Roberts's excellent series of picture books. They show Swansea's Slip Bridge in its heyday, when it formed a popular link between the sands of Swansea Bay and the floral delights of Victoria Park. As I write this foreword, the bridge has been recently moved to a new home on the city's promenade, an unhappy compromise between two opposing points of view, either in favour of expensively restoring it in its original setting, or scrapping it altogether.

Readers will find other familiar landmarks, many now gone, contained in the pages of this book. They will decide for themselves if the city is the better for their passing.

We are indebted to David for his diligence and industry in gathering another collection of scenes that will stimulate the memory and doubtlessly provoke some debate. The Evening Post applauds his achievement.

Spencer Feeney
Editor
South Wales Evening Post

A fitting salute

THE briefest of glances at 21st Century Swansea is evidence enough that the people and places within its city and county boundary are changing at a pace faster than ever before in its long and proud history and on almost every front.

Right now it is not only Wales's first and finest seaside city and the Principality's premier waterside location, it is also one of ongoing development in a bid to retain its mantle as both a prominent business centre and an incomparable visitor hotspot.

The changes that will carry Swansea confidently forward into the future are happening before our very eyes. There is barely a day when the city skyline doesn't alter in one way or another, particularly that part of it within the grasp of developers involved in the exciting SA1 scheme along the city's eastern gateway.

All this — and more — is happening before us and visibly so. Other changes, however, have crept up unnoticed, often leaving no time to say farewell to what existed before. It is here, by refreshing the memory that the pictures in this book earn their keep.

Much has been written about Swansea, its origins, early history and the derivation of its name. That is best left to the academics. This book focuses on some of the more recent social aspects of the modern city and the surrounding area. It helps to keep alive how its streets once were, provide some clues to the kind of people who walked them and shows the kind of activities they indulged in — those things closest to their hearts.

Swansea – Thank you for the days will carry all those things forward, a fitting salute to a proud city with a proud heritage.

David Roberts, 2005.

City streetscapes

The central area and clocktower of the market established in Swansea in the 1830s, pictured shortly before its demolition in 1896.

The view up Temple Street, towards Castle Street, 1893. The street was one of many which vanished under the city centre rebuilding programme that followed the devastation of bombing in the Second World War.

Oxford Street, viewed towards the castle in the late 1880s showing The Globe Inn, Teague's shop and, on the right, the market.

Picton Place looking towards St. Helen's Road, 1920. On the left is the Swansea and South Wales Institute for the Blind. The building was demolished in 1930 and replaced by the Plaza Cinema. This is now The Kingsway.

Built in 1897, this was the imposing arched exterior of Swansea Market, Oxford Street, in 1900. The twin towers marked the impressive main entrance. The baskets on the heavily laden cart seem none too safe.

Waterloo Street was another that fell victim to German wartime bombing. This store advertisement for Morgan Jenkins, shows how some of its buildings looked around 1900.

A busy view of High Street, 1905. The Lewis Lewis store, founded in 1866 is prominent on a street that was then mainly cobbled. There was still plenty of horse manure on the road even though, by then, the trams had been converted to run on electricity instead of horse power. Peglers the grocers can be seen on the right.

Swansea Free Library in Alexandra Road, 1905. The former police station that adjoined the left hand side of the building had yet to be built when this scene, complete with tram and horse-drawn transport, was captured.

A very busy Wind Street, about 1900, heavily congested with people and horse-drawn vehicles, at a time when it was the commercial centre of the town. Most of these buildings still exist today, but now as bars and pubs rather than their original use as home to businesses and financial institutions.

The tram terminus at High Street, opposite the Hotel Cameron, 1905.

The tram wires that once spread their web around Swansea and some of its developing districts can clearly be seen in this street scene of 1905 which shows Swansea Library.

This was how Castle Street looked until 1908 when the buildings on both sides here were demolished to make a wider thoroughfare linking High Street with Wind Street.

Oxford Street on a busy summertime shopping day in 1911, looking towards Temple Street with its original David Evans store building. The centre of the street was taken up with tramlines.

Looking along Gower Street, 1910. This later became The Kingsway and the impressive building on the right is Mount Pleasant Baptist Chapel, still there today.

The Bay View Hotel at the junction of Oystermouth Road and St Helen's Road, 1910. At this point Swansea's tramway system met up with the Mumbles Railway.

The Three Lamps Hotel, Temple Street, destroyed in 1941 during the Three Nights Blitz. The name alone rose from the ashes and adorned a popular hostelry opposite this site for many years.

Swansea Guildhall, Somerset Place , 1920. Today the canon-guarded memorial statue of John Hussey Vivian has been relocated in the Maritime Quarter and the building is more familiar as the Dylan Thomas Centre.

High Street railway station as it looked in 1920.

The Slip Bridge which carried pedestrians over Mumbles Road, the track of the Mumbles Railway and the LMS Swansea Victoria to Shrewsbury railway line, as it appeared in 1920. It now rests on Swansea promenade.

Basking in all its early glory and enhanced by the summertime splendour of Victoria Park, Swansea's Slip Bridge, in the early 1920s. It was a much used link between the nearby sands and the gardens for day trippers.

Looking up Wind Street, in the 1920s, before completion of the popular Ben Evans store that stood where Castle Square is today. It was destroyed by wartime German bombers in the Three Nights' Blitz of 1941.

Dilwyn Street, 1925. The Bishopston bus is flanked on the right by a tram, and on the left a horse-drawn carriage — both contenders for passengers in those heady days.

The old Swan Hotel, Gower Street, 1925.

The Royal Institution of South Wales — Swansea Museum — looking much the same in 1930 as it does today.

Swansea's main police station, at the junction of Alexandra Road and Orchard Street, 1930.

The Glynn Vivian art gallery, Alexandra Road, 1930.

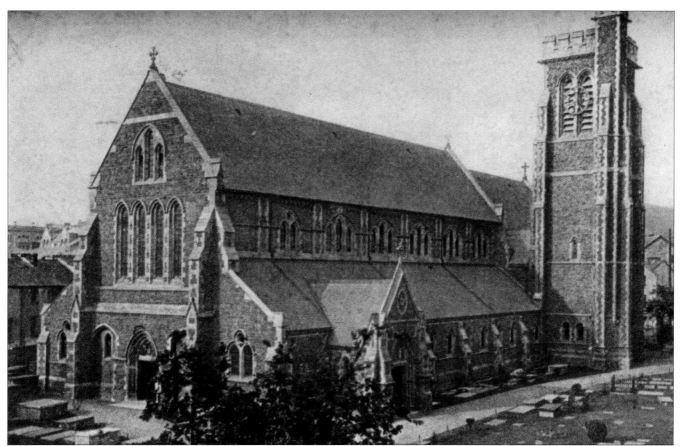

St Mary's Parish Church, mid-1930s. It was destroyed by wartime bombing in 1941 and later rebuilt before being re-opened to worshippers in 1959.

The Cenotaph on the promenade opposite the Recreation Ground, 1930.

Swansea General and Eye Hospital sandwiched between St Helen's Road and Phillips Parade, 1930.

The Patti Pavilion had only recently been moved from Craig y Nos Castle in the Swansea Valley, to Victoria Park as a gift of opera singer Adelina Patti, late 1920s.

Temple Street, 1930, with the original David Evans' store building on the left. It was destroyed by wartime bombing in the Three Nights Blitz of 1941.

A very empty and tree-lined Walter Road, 1930.

St James's Gardens, just off upper Walter Road, 1930.

The square between High Street Station and the Grand Hotel, 1930s.

Walter Road, early 1930s. the car in the foreground is heading towards Uplands.

Looking up Temple Street towards Castle Street, May 1933, towards the Evening Post building and the castle.

The impressive Oxford Street facade of the market, 1935.

Castle Street viewed from its junction with Temple Street and Castle Bailey, mid-1930s.

A tranquil view of Swansea Guildhall captured in late 1930s.

The floral clock near the Guildhall, late-1930s. It was always a popular attraction with locals and visitors alike.

These two cannons which were displayed in the forecourt of Swansea Guildhall — Now the Dylan Thomas Centre — were trophies from the Crimean War. This picture was taken in 1935.

The Morgan Jenkins & Son warehouse, Rutland Street, 1950.

York Street roundabout at the bottom of Princess Way, mid-1960s. The derelict building is Burrows Lodge which became railway offices.

Princess Way, Swansea, in the mid-1950s. The building on the left was occupied by Boots the Chemist.

Looking up Green Dragon Lane, from the Strand towards Wind Street, early 1950s.

An interesting view eastwards across the back of houses in Graham Street, Hafod over Neath Road and past a former storage depot towards St Thomas, early 1950s.

Lower Union Street, with the market on the right and Peter Jones's restaurant on the left, mid-1960s.

Looking up High Street from its junction with College Street, towards the former Lewis Lewis store, late 1950s.

Courts Furnishers dominates this view across The Kingsway roundabout, mid-1950s.

Looking across The Kingsway roundabout from College Street to Belle Vue Way, mid-1960s. Orchard Street is on the right. The modern day pedestrian subway system had yet to be built.

An aerial view of Swansea city centre, May 1961. Much redevelopment has taken place since and many of the buildings seen here have vanished.

Looking towards the Kingsway, from the direction of Orchard Street, 1954. The Dragon Hotel is there now.

An early view of Castle Gardens, 1953. Its shrubs and trees had yet to attain their full glory.

This late 1950s Oxford Street scene will hold memories for many. On the left is the Co-operative House building, while on the right can be seen British Home Stores, tailors Weaver to Wearer, Tom Evans the jewellers, Phillips electrical store and Marks & Spencer.

A view from the Slip Bridge, showing Swansea Baths Laundry on the left at the junction of St Helen's Road and Oystermouth Road, 1969.

Many cheered the fact that the Dragon Hotel regained its original name in 2005. This is a bird's eye view of how the building, The Kingsway, left, and Belle Vue Way, right, looked in the early 1970s.

A spectacular panorama across Swansea from the east side, in the 1950s. Much of what can bee seen here has now vanished and in its place have risen up the city centre, maritime quarter and SA1 developments. The picture was taken from Kilvey Hill with St. Thomas and Maesteg Park in the foreground. The two clearly visible gasometers stand on a site now occupied by Tesco's Oystermouth Road store.

Princess Way looking up towards The Kingsway roundabout, 1971. The store on the left was occupied by Boots the Chemists while David Evans is on the right, along with Castle Gardens.

Looking down on Princess Way and The Kingsway roundabout, now a concrete bowl rather than city centre oasis, of floral colour and natural greenery, late 1970s. The roundabout was excavataed to make way for pedestrian subways.

Oxford Street, showing Oxford buildings and the Carlton Cinema with its twin towers, around 1978, after it ceased to operate as a cinema. It was later converted to house Waterstones bookstore.

A view across Swansea centre towards the River Tawe and docks beyond, with Port Talbot in the distance, early 1980s. A Tesco store now stands in the vicinity of the gasholder frames and the Vetch Field is to the right.

A moment in time. Showing 10.30am precisely, this animated Quadrant Shopping Centre clock, caused many a shopper to pause as it chimed into action in the early 1980s.

The waterfalls that once decorated the side of Swansea Leisure Centre. They were later drained and used as a skateboard area and later still the greenery alongside became a car park.

The David Evans store, Princess Way, looking out over Castle Gardens, in the late 1960s. The store closed on Saturday January 15, 2005. It had been a feature of Swansea life for 105 years.

No barrage on the River Tawe when this early 1990s view was captured. The BT tower — before it received its reflective glass and the original Sainsbury's supermarket building can be seen.

The South Dock marina, looking landwards, during the snow of 1982 with the floating pub and restaurant, The Picton Sea Eagle, in the background. It was later moved from the city to Liverpool.

The British Transport Docks Board offices, at the junction of Adelaide Street and Somerset Place, 1980s — now it has been lavishly restyled as the five star Morgan's Hotel.

Looking down a busy Oxford Street, from Princess Way, with the aid of a telephoto camera lens, 1983.

Castle Gardens and the now closed David Evans store, 1989.

An aerial view of a rapidly changing Swansea city centre, mid-1980s. Among clearly visible landmarks are County Hall, at the foot of the picture; the arched glass roof of the market, the Quadrant Shopping Centre, below it and, in the bottom left hand corner, Swansea prison.

The mouth of the River Tawe before construction of the barrage, early 1990s.

St John Ambulance Brigade stalwart
Will Nicholls, of Gowerton, with his
two sons, early 1920s.

A training exercise mounted by members of Waunarlwydd St. John Ambulance Brigade members in the 1920s.

Cyril Dicks and Doreen Smale who were married at Fleet Street Congregational Church on May 1, 1943. They are pictured here with their bridesmaids and flower girls.

Members of the Glanmor Club during a get-together, 1950.

This group is pictured on the steps of Swansea Guildhall before embarking on an exchange visit to Recklinghausen, Germany, arranged by Mrs Frances Matthews in 1951.

Brynymor Traders Association members at a dinner during the mid-1950s.

Chief guests, including Mayor, Sir William Jenkins at the annual ball of Swansea Borough police force, 1948.

Members of Swansea Women's Guild, who met at the Heathfield Club, all dressed up in a western theme for an event in the early 1950s.

A civic gathering, possibly a retirement, attended by Leslie Drew, former director of education, late 1950s.

Mr Ernest Davies presented a Swansea China dessert service to the Glynn Vivian art gallery at an informal tea party held by the Swansea art galleries committee there, 1956. Mr Davies is seated second from the left, along with Councillor H Libby, Mayor of Swansea; Mrs C F Nicholson Mayoress and Mr Sidney Heath.

Students and lecturers of Swansea College of Art, 1956. Included are a number of well known local artists.

A group of friends enjoy a night out at the Pier Hotel, Mumbles, 1959.

Brothers and sisters of the Dymond Family, Danygraig, Port Tennant, 1960.

A civic handshake at the official opening of the Pioneer Youth Club at the Vivian Hall, Blackpill, 1960.

Some of the regulars with the steward and stewardess at The Heathfield Club, 1960.

Employees of motor delear and car repairers Oscar Chess, Gloucester Place, all set for a night out, 1962.

A fete held in aid of St James's Church, Walter Road, Swansea, Thursday, November 4, 1965.

A presentation at a special staff gathering to mark the centenary of the Lewis Lewis, High Street department store in the 1960s.

These were some of the visitors to the first fair held at Kilvey Church for 30 years on October 6, 1966.

Rain failed to dampen the spirits of these visitors to a summer fete at Killay House, National Childrens' Home, Killay, in the late 1960s.

Members of Brynymor Road Traders Association look on as their chairman, jeweller and watch repairer Charles Dilley makes a presentation to the Mayor and Mayoress, late 1960s.

Crowds gather at the National
Children's Home, Killay
House fete, 1970.

Youngsters try their hand at beating Swansea City goalkeeper Tony Millington at a garden fete at Killay House National Children's Home, Killay, one Saturday early in June, 1970.

Visitors brave the rain to watch one of the attractions at the annual fete at the Killay House National Children's Home, Killay, 1972.

Children of members of the Armine Social Club, Fforestfach, off to a pantomime at the Grand Theatre, 1973.

Successful Mumbles and Gower advanced Cub Scout badge leaders after receiving their awards, 1974.

Townhill and Mayhill Camera Club members at their annual awards night 1979.

Lord Mayor of Swansea Lillian Hopkin heads dignitaries at the Swansea Chamber of Trade window dressing competition awards, 1986.

Members of the Rotary Club of Swansea, at one of their regular meetings, 1982.

Reverend Ann Lewis, curate of St Mary's Church, assists parishioners at the church fete, in the early 1980s. The construction of a new Littlewoods store for the city is underway behind.

Swansea Rugby Club players, including Paul Arnold, knocking over a pile of pennies built up by regulars at the Star Inn, Carmarthen Road, Fforestfach.

A civic hand for the lucky ticket at a members coffee morning fund raiser of the Inner Wheel Club of Swansea at the Mansion House, 1989.

District diary

Charlie Cockings
outside his home at
28 Vivian Street,
Hafod, overlooked
by Hafod Tip, 1927.

A group of women taking a walk alongside Clyne Valley Woods, 1907.

The school at Parkmill Gower, 1908. The Gower Inn is just visible on the right.

The old bridge, Gorseinon, 1912.

The Cwm, Landore, with Morris Castle just visible at the top of the hill in the background, 1920. The mine building in the centre is the Cwm pit. The posts mark the route of the tramway which terminated at Cwm Level Road where St Peter's Catholic Church stands.

View of Townhill, west of Hill Farm, 1929.

The fountain at Cwmdonkin Park, Uplands in full flow, 1930.

Townhill Road, Sketty, late 1930s.

In the days before Neath River Bridge at Briton Ferry this bus was heading for Margam, Port Talbot, by the only way it could — via Morriston and Neath. Here it is seen in Cwm Road, Bonymaen, about 1930.

Theopilus and Katherine Jones, proprietors of the Manor Bakery, at 68 Manor Road, Manselton, 1930s.

The children's paddling pool, Brynmill Park, early 1930s.

Morris Lane School, viewed from the back of Mackworth Terrace, St Thomas, looking towards Swansea, 1935.

The ornate Swiss chalet cottage at Singleton Park, mid-1930s.

Local authority housing in Gors Avenue, Townhill, 1937.

Gomer Road, Townhill, mid-1920s.

The Grange, West Cross, 1941. It was used as a Territorial Army centre before being demolished to make way for the building that exists there today.

Until the opening of the Fabian Way dual carriageway this low bridge on Swansea's eastern approach was a hindrance to high sided traffic. It is seen here in the 1950s.

A young Hafod boy in the lane behind Gerald Street and Aberdyberthi Street, Hafod, in 1942. In the background is the former Hafod Tip, now the site of Pentrehafod Comprehensive School.

Looking towards Swansea along Fabian Way, still under construction, mid-1950s.

The Bridge Inn, St. Thomas, alongside the docks entrance early 1950s.

A view across Cockett, early 1950s.

St John's Church, Woodfield Street, Morriston, 1950s.

The Blue Bell Inn, Waun Wen, late 1950s.

Brynymor Road, in the mid-1970s.

Two likely lads enjoy
a spot of fun in
Vivian Road, Sketty,
1963.

Cwm Road, looking towards Hafod Bridge and Prince of Wales Road, from the Brynmelyn flats, mid-1960s.

The Uplands Hotel, Uplands Crescent, early 1980s.

Local authority homes at Townhill,
viewed from Cwmbwrla, mid-1980s.

Evelyn Road, Mayhill, almost impassable after a heavy snowfall in 1982.

Warren Kelly's shop at the corner of Lion Street and Carmarthen Road, in Waun Wen, mid-1960s.

Crowds watch as workmen make safe the remains of Hafod School the morning after it was severely damaged by fire, on the night of March 5, 1992.

Notts Gardens, Cwmdonkin, after a heavy snowfall in 1982.

Parties and parades

Dressing a float for Swansea east side carnival, 1936.

The Princess Royal at a Guide Rally in Singleton Park, mid-1930s.

Residents of Meusydd Road, Landore, celebrate the Coronation of King George V, 1937.

A Christmas cake baked by Ben Presdee, of Mumbles, for a children's party at RAF Fairwood, 1943. It had the RAF insignia on it.

Sunday School children of St Barnabus' Church Christmas tea party, December 7, 1938.

Ynystawe Carnival Queen and her attendants 1945.

Residents of Sydney Street, Brynhyfryd, celebrate VE Day, May 8 1945.

A Christmas party at RAF Fairwood, for local children, 1943.

Wilks music shop in Oxford Street, was the focus for VJ Day celebrations in 1945. Pictured are residents and children from neighbouring homes in the street.

Residents of Campbell Street and North Hill, Mount Pleasant, united for a party to celebrate VE Day, 1945.

Residents of Garden Street, Orange Street, Grenfell Street, Kynaston Place, St David's Place, and Rutland Street, came together to celebrate VE Day, 1945.

Residents of Thomas Row, Dyffaty, at a street party to celebrate VJ Day, August 1945.

Members of the Glanmor Club, Sketty, enjoy themselves at a New Year's Eve party, 1947.

Staff of R M Douglas construction at a Christmas party, late 1940s.

Staff of Macowards, Oxford Street store, at a dinner in the Pier Hotel, Mumbles, 1948.

Handing out gifts at a children's Christmas party organised by Swansea police at the Brangwyn Hall, 1950s.

Members of Clyne Golf Club at a dinner dance, early 1950s.

Laden with presents, children of employees of the ICI works, Landore, enjoy their Christmas party, 1950.

Youngsters from Manselton, at a Festival of Britain fancy dress party, 1951.

Something special must have been captivating the attention of these children at a Christmas party held in the canteen of the ICI works at Landore, 1951.

Staff of Macowards Oxford Street store, at a dinner at the Langland Bay Hotel, March 5, 1952.

Coronation Day celebrations at Rodney Street, Sandfields, June 1953.

Residents of Tymawr Street, Port Tennant, celebrate the Coronation of Queen Elizabeth II in style, June, 1953.

Workers of the Corona soft drinks factory, Kingsway, Fforestfach, their families and children at a party there, 1955.

Women workers from the slider section of the ICI Waunarlwydd zip factory at their Christmas dinner held at the Mackworth Hotel, High Street, December 23, 1959.

Ted and June Elsey, of Recorder Street, Sandfields, at a special romantic evening out dinner they won in a local newspaper competition, 1960s.

A Ruby Wedding anniversary party for Lil and Cyril, mine hosts of the Cross Keys pub, St Mary Street, mid-1960s.

Members of the Uplands Arts Club held a fancy dress party at the home of their president Councillor Herbert T Morgan and Mrs Morgan, mid-1960s.

Office staff of the Mettoy toy factory, Fforestfach, at their Christmas Party, 1965.

Swansea Hospital Children's Ball, 1966.

Women regulars of the Globe Inn, Landore, at their annual dinner and dance at the Coopers Arms, Landore, Friday, November 11, 1966.

Children of Watkin Street, Mount Pleasant, during celebrations to mark the Investiture of the Prince of Wales, 1969.

Staff of Hodges Menswear at the firm's annual dance, late 1960s.

Swansea Firemen's Ball at the Dolphin Hotel, Whitewalls, 1970.

Food hall staff of David Evans store let their hair down at a party, 1975.

Fancy dress was the order of the day for these residents of Grenfell Park during celebrations to mark the Silver Jubilee of Queen Elizabeth II, July 1977.

There was plenty to eat and fun for all when residents of Grenfell Park celebrated the Silver Jubilee of Queen Elizabeth II, July 1977.

Younger days

A young girl takes her dolls for a pram ride in the back garden of her home in Pyle Road, Bishopston, 1944.

A group of smartly dressed young boys outside a Swansea house, early 1920s. One is holding a football so were they perhaps members of a local team?

Youngsters at a Clydach youth club intensely scrutinise a game of chess, late 1940s.

The 1st Manselton (St Michael's) Guide Company in Singleton Park, with Guide captain Joan Tainsh with Audrey Mawson standing next to her, 1950.

Cadle Brownie pack, about 1954.

A young boy proudly poses with his tricycle outside his home in Cockett Road, 1941.

Three young members of the Presdee family on a hayrick — Gladys, Arthur and Alice, 1915.

St James's Guide troop members during their summer annual camp at Llanmadoc, Gower, 1955.

Akela Paddie Leckie with members of the Cub Scout pack attached to Our Lady of Lourdes Church, Townhill, proudly hold their flag aloft, late 1950s.

Three youngsters dressed up in their 'Sunday best' outside the Cross Keys Inn, St. Mary Street, 1957.

Children at Killay House children's home, Killay, busy themselves wrapping presents, Christmas 1958.

Young girls show off their best dresses at a hospital ball at the Brangwyn Hall, 1958.

Young fans flock to get the autograph of Radio One DJ Keith Skues at the Top Rank, Kingsway, mid 1960s. He was just one of a number of personalities at the event.

Visitors — young and old — at the Christmas toy fair at the David Evans department store, November 22, 1965.

Two young girls enjoy sun, sea and sand at Swansea Beach, 1952.

Roundabout fun in the park at Southend, Mumbles, in the summer of 1968.

Children at Killay House children's home, Killay, explore the delights of camping, late 1960s.

A giant jigsaw competition underway during a summer fete at Killay House children's home, Killay, early 1970s.

A lesson in telling the time perhaps, for these youngsters at Victoria Park's floral clock in the early 1970s.

Some of the gang from Siloh Road, Landore, 1972.

Transport for baby 1948-style. A proud aunt and her niece take a break on Swansea promenade.

Members of the 42nd Fforestfach, Scout troop receiving Chief Scout awards from their district commisioner at the Scout Hall, Carmarthen Road, 1984.

Mumbles and Gower

A group of children at the roadside in Murton in the late 1890s.

Three Cliffs Bay, early 1900s.

Limeslade Bay, Mumbles early 1900s.

Walkers enjoy the delights of the cliff path at Langland, early 1900s.

A band plays as crowds throng Mumbles Pier on a summer weekend in the early 1900s.

Clearly a crowd puller, this was the 'figure of eight' rollercoaster at Oystermouth, 1904.

Murton village looking towards the Plough and Harrow pub in the distance, 1905.

The Bishopston Valley Hotel, early 1900s.

Beachgoers at Rotherslade Bay, early 1950s.

Caswell Bay, early 1950s.

Caswell Bay at high tide, early 1950s.

Rotherslade Bay, with Langland around the headland, early 1950s.

The pub, left, and houses on the village green at Llangennith early 1950s.

An unusual view of Mumbles Pier across some of the rooftops of Southend, early 1950s.

Fortes Ice cream parlour on the corner of the Dunns, Oystermouth, 1971.

Southend, Mumbles, after a heavy snowfall, 1982.

Looking down Newton Road, Mumbles, after the snow of 1982.

A picturesque Langland Bay in the snow, 1982.

A snowbound Southend, Mumbles, early 1982.

Days out

Swansea families enjoy a day's outing on a Gower beach, 1910.

A Sunday School trip from Waun Wen
to Porthcawl, 1930.

People enjoyed having
their photographs taken
on this small horse and
cart situated opposite the
Big Apple, Mumbles,
1942.

Crowds throng Swansea Sands near the Slip Bridge, 1930.

A party of friends set to enjoy the delights of Ilfracombe after a paddle steamer crossing from Swansea.

An apprentices' day out from the John Evans Foundry, Morriston, 1946.

Rubber band powered aircraft models flying around a pole at a hobbies exhibition in the Patti Pavilion which attracted over 15,000 visitors in just four days, October, 1948.

Staff of the Morgan Jenkins wholesale drapery, pictured near the water chute at Coney Beach funfair during an outing to Porthcawl, 1950.

Staff of the Lewis Lewis store, High Street, all set for an outing to Llandrindod Wells with principals of the company Gwyneth Lewis — in floral dress — and Herbert Lewis. It was a Thursday half day in the mid-1950s.

A group of Swansea women were enjoying a day out in Mumbles during the early 1950s when they stopped to have their photograph taken on this wooden horse which was a familiar part of the scene there then.

An outing by regulars of the Belle Vue pub, now the Quadrant Gate, 1948. All the people were good friends and

neighbours of mainly Garden Street, Orange Street, Grenfell Street, Thomas Row and Wellington Street.

Staff of the South Wales Electricity Board's Strand depot all set for a day out in the mid-1950s.

Everything bar the kitchen sink — it was all packed for this day on the beach near the Slip, mid-1950s.

Employees of the South Wales Transport bus company often conveyed people on day trips. On this occasion the passengers were their own children — all set for a jaunt to Porthcawl, 1952.

Staff of J&P Bevan ready to depart on their annual outing to Aberystwyth, 1953.

A youngster enjoys the freedom of Swansea Beach near the Slip, mid-1950s.

Two young lads on a day out at the Gower Show, Penrice, 1954.

With the old beach tents behind them, this Swansea family was snapped while relaxing on their deckchairs during a summer's day at Langland Bay, 1956.

Swansea Telegram messenger boys on a day out to Barry Island, July 31, 1957.

Staff of the Louis Marx toy company ready for a day out at the races, early 1960s.

Swansea Corporation staff didn't let rain spoil their fun on this outing to Weston Super Mare, early 1960s.

Men from Port Tennant all set for a flutter at the races, early 1960s.

A group of Townhill women enjoy a knees up on a break at a Butlins holiday camp, during the 1960s.

A United Welsh Services coach carried these steelworks boilermen on a day out, 1963. They are pictured at Sway Road, Morriston, before setting off.

Members of Cwmfelin Social Club all set for an annual day out, early 1970s.

Office staff of the Prudential Assurance Company at Swansea during a London visit, mid-1970s.

A group of staff at David Evans store all set for a day out, mid-1970s.

Waterside ways

Capturing the view from Knab
Rock, Mumbles, late 1930s.

The paddle steamer Lady Moyra leaving the River Tawe
packed with people for an evening cruise early 1930s.

The high level railway bridge has rolled back on itself to allow this vessel, The Cognac, to enter the North Dock.
Weaver's mill is in the background, 1920s.

The Swansea trawler Radnor Castle undergoing repairs in the dry dock alongside Pockett's Wharf, 1920s.

The Winterhude, a German grain carrier, discharging at Weaver's flour mill in the North Dock basin, 1935.

Two vessels moored alongside the ice factory on the eastern quayside of the River Tawe 1935. The new Sail Bridge slices across the river at this point now.

A vessel passing through the Kings Dock lock, aided by a tug, early 1960s.

A 1960s aerial view of the dry docks at Kings Dock.

Swansea trawlers at Prince of Wales Dock, late 1970s.

HMS Vidals helicopter lands on deck while the vessel is moored at Swansea Docks, 1959.

Crowds of well-wishers — mostly parents — lined the quayside to wave their children off on a voyage aboard the educational cruise ship Devonia as she eased her way through the lock at Swansea Docks with a full compliment of schoolchildren. They were embarking on a trip to the Mediterranean, mid 1960s.

A view across Swansea Docks, around 1936.

Three tug boats busy themselves ministering to the needs of two freighters in King's Dock, 1955.

Two landmarks vital to seamen in Swansea Bay — Mumbles lighthouse and, alongside the pier, the RNLI's Mumbles lifeboat station. The tide was at its lowest ebb when this 1964 picture was taken.

That's entertainment

Sisters Maureen and Marian Bruton, members of Swansea
East Jazz Band, at Maesteg Park, St Thomas, 1952.

A group of youngsters who took part in Mumbles carnival, 1931.

A crowd outside the Carlton Cinema, Oxford Street, 1931. They were waiting to see the Jack Holt film *Fifty Fathoms Deep*. The commisionaire keeping them in order was Joe Hildritch.

The Modernettes, a group of young performers, in a practice session with Raie Copp and a colleague, 1951.

Manselton Senior Girls School choir, with music teacher Hazel Evans 1952.

A combined Swansea School Choir on
the steps of the Brangwyn Hall, 1955.

Manselton Male Voice Choir, 1955.

The principal ladies of Swansea Amateur Operatic Society's production of The Dancing Years, 1959.

Mae Zetterling interviewed by a TV reporter during location shooting above Cwmbwrla for the film Only Two Can Play, much of which was filmed in Swansea. One of the Cwmfelin stacks can be seen in the background, 1962.

Peter Sellers filming Only Two Can Play in the Kingsway with the YMCA building in the background,1962.

Girls from Powys Avenue School, Townhill, who had performed a sketch entitled Hiawatha at the Urdd eisteddfod at Singleton Park, 1963. The energetic young man was apparently just passing by when he demonstrated his athletic skills, much to their delight.

A Scout and Guide Gang Show at the Grand Theatre during the early 1970s.

Music time at Killay House fete, Killay, 1970s.

Youngsters of Gendros Infants School during their Nativity performance, Christmas 1976.

Gendros School PTA pantomime at Dilwyn Llewellyn School, Cockett, now Dylan Thomas school, 1981.

Pupils of Terrace Road School, during one of their Christmas plays, 1985.

Right on track

Double decker Swansea tramcar No 33 travels along Oxford Street heading for Brynmill, 1909.

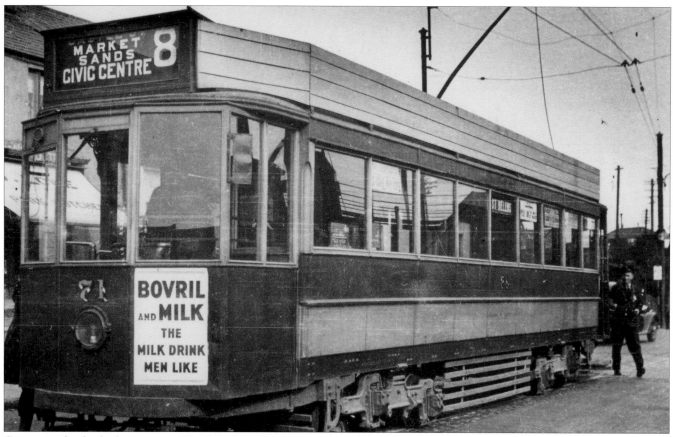

Swansea single decker tramcar No 71at Port Tennant, early 1900s. It is all set to head back into town.

The Mumbles Train at Brynmill station in the days when it was hauled by steam power, 1910. The centre carriage was converted from a battery powered car that proved unsuccessful.

Boarding the Mumbles Train at Rutland Street, for a bank holiday jaunt to the pier, 1910.

A former Rhondda and Swansea Bay Railway locomotive hauling coal wagons at Prince of Wales Dock junction near Swansea East Dock station, mid-1920s.

A Beyer-Garratt locomotive in use at the Vivian copper works in the late 1920s. It was bought to negotiate the tight bends on the track inside the works and also the use of two locomotives on the gradient up to the GWSR sidings.

A single deck tram at the Brynhyfryd terminus, about 1925. Cars like this were in regular use on the route in and out of Swansea.

Inside the tram depot at St Helen's Road, late 1920s. Today the site is occupied by Swansea Crown Court.

Swansea Bay Station, near St Helen's sports ground, mid-1960s. By this time the Swansea Victoria rail line had closed and wind-blown sand was doing its bit to reclaim the trackbed.

The Mumbles Train near Ashleigh Road on its final day of operation, January 5, 1960.

Upper Bank locomotive sheds, December 2, 1961.

A steam-hauled railway special at High Street station in September 1965. A Diesel Multiple Unit can be seen in the background.

Entering High Street station, about 1966 is diesel hydraulic locomotive Western Hussar. The locomotives were among British Rail's workhorses after the demise of steam power.

Upper Bank, Pentrechwyth, locomotive depot of the Swansea Vale Railway mid-1950s.

A group of young railway enthusiasts pick up some tips for the future from the driver of a Paddington-bound locomotive 5037 at High Street, Station, late 1950s.

Lessons in life

Pupils dressed as colliers at Graig
Infants School, Morriston, 1937.

Some of the pupils at St Thomas Boys School, with headmaster Mr Davies and teacher Mr Rees, 1928.

Terrace Road School won the Swansea Schools Sports Shield in 1933. Here some of the pupils proudly display their trophy.

Class six at Baptist Well Council School, Waun Wen, 1925.

St Thomas Girls School class 3B, 1928.

Pupils of Plasmarl Junior School, 1931-32.

A class at Plasmarl Infants School, 1936.

Oxford Street Girls School Junior Red Cross team, 1938.

Students and lecturers at Clarke's College, 1939.

Terrace Road School scholarship class, 1936.

A class at Manselton Boys School, 1948.

St Thomas
Junior School,
June 5, 1952.

Form 1C
Dynevor
School, 1953.

Pupils and staff at Dumbarton House School, 1953.

Bishopston Boys Junior School pupils, 1955.

Bishopston Girls Junior School pupils, 1955.

Pupils of Lonlas Junior School ready to perform at the 1957 Urdd National eisteddfod, held in North Wales.

A class at Mynyddbach Girls School, 1957.

Some of the pupils at Manselton School, 1955.

The wooden school buildings of Glanmor School for Girls, mid-1950s.

A class at Dunvant Junior Mixed School, early 1960s.

Pupils at Brynhyfryd School during St David's Day 1962.

Pupils of Gendros Primary School on a sponsored jog to raise funds after the school was gutted by fire, July 1981.

Powys Avenue Junior School pupils, 1961.

On the move

Two young men proudly show off their new Mini in the Kingsway outside what is now
the site of the Gwalia Housing Association Offices, 1962.

A young Griff Jeffreys at Dunvant's Killan Colliery, early 1900s. Griff's father used to haul coal and goods for the colliery up to the former Swansea Victoria to Shrewsbury railway line at Dunvant. The picture was taken near today's Dunvant Square.

One of the steam wagons used by the Jeffreys brothers in their early 1900s Three Crosses haulage business. The company used to supply pit props to Dunvant Colliery and other local businesses and was the start of the Jeffreys Commercial Motors business that later flourished at Plasmarl. The firm's telephone number was Three Crosses No 4. Griff Jeffreys is the one with the cigarette.

A South Wales Transport, AEC K-Type, open-top double decker bus at the company's Brunswick Street depot, 1925.

A Dodge van operated by Graig Confectionery at Lon Coed Bran, Sketty, 1937.

A group of drivers who worked for Streamline Taxis with one of their vehicles, 1938. The firm operated from a base in the railway arches that ran alongside Victoria Road.

One of the vehicles pressed into service as an ambulance at Manselton ambulance depot, during the Three Nights Blitz of February 1941, with some of those who helped crew it.

Famous racing car builder and driver Colin Chapman in a Mk 8, streamline Lotus racing car at Fairwood Airport during a motor racing meeting in 1954. It was a predecessor of the famous, all-conquering Lotus 11 cars.

Firemen from Blue Watch at Mumbles Fire Station on one of the last trips they made aboard the now restored fire appliance ACY 463 — known as the Big Six, 1965.

They say the sun always shone in years gone by, but this picture proves different. It shows a typical wet shopping day in The Kingsway, during the mid-1960s. Many once familiar stores can be seen including the long gone clothing mecca of C&A.

This collection of motor vehicles was snapped on the day of the sale of The Orchards, Barlands, near Kittle, during early April, 1965. It certainly shows some of the cars that were on our roads at the time.

A Morton Air Services De Havilland Heron aircraft on the apron at Fairwood Airport, preparing for a flight to Jersey, 1967.

This mobile shop used to travel around Swansea's housing estates and did very well dispensing meat for the Co-op Freezer Centre, Fforestfach, in the 1960s.

Working at it

A crane and its driver at the Millbrook works, Landore, 1950s.

Members of Swansea Constabulary, pre-1904.

Boilermen at King's Dock, 1920s.

Locals from The Cwm, Landore, going through coal slurry in the hunt for fuel during the 1920s depression.

Brothers Will, Bert, Fred and Syd Wayne, on the formation of the Limited Company in 1930. They went on to give Swansea its first taste of supermarket shopping at their Uplands Store — Waynes.

Workmen at the Cwmfelin steelworks, Cwmbwrla, 1930.

Steelworkers at the Cwmfelin steelworks, June 19, 1937.

Meet B Company of the 14th (Glamorgan) Swansea Home Guard, early 1940s.

Cwmfelin steelworks employees Tommy Francis, engine driver; and a young lad — both standing on the locomotive — with shunter Eddie Trick, 1940s.

A barmaid pulls a refreshing pint at the Ivorites Hotel, High Street, at a Christmastime in the early 1950s.

Bus conductor Bernard Phillips and his wife Joyce pictured in front of the South Wales Transport AEC bus he worked between Morriston and Sketty. The picture was taken in 1946 on the site of what is now the Dragon Hotel, Belle Vue Way.

Two United Welsh Bus Company drivers and their conductors take a break at their terminus near the Gwyn Arms, near Abercrave in the Upper Swansea Valley, 1950.

Excavation underway for the construction of foundations for Velindre Tinplate Works, 1949.

Construction of the foundations for the main part of Velindre tinplate works, November 24, 1949.

A bus cleaner at South Wales Transport's Brunswick Street depot.

South Wales Electricity Board managers and apprentices at the company's Strand, depot, 1955.

Students at Swansea College of Art Teacher Training department, 1956.

Workers at the Atlas Sprinkler works, Fforestfach, late 1950s.

Office staff at Signode, Fforestfach, 1959.

A barmaid at the Old York pub, opposite the New York pub, Princess Way, 1963.

Some of the yard staff and drivers at the Freightliner depot, Crymlyn Burrows, on the day it was officially opened, January 1, 1970.

Delivery crew and shop floor staff at the South Wales Electricity Board's, Pontarddulais works, mid-1970s.

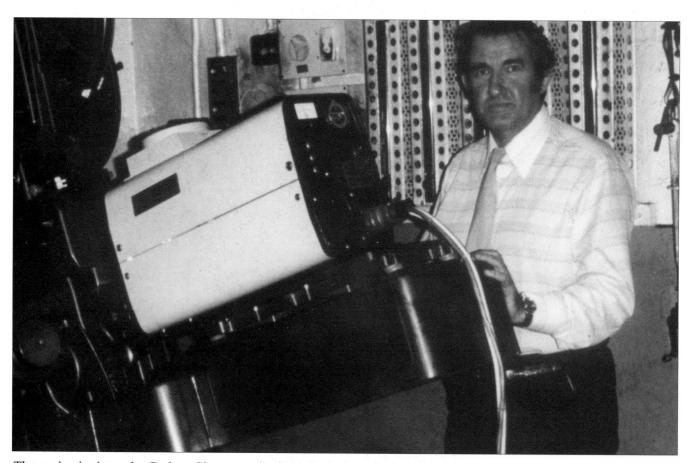

The projectionist at the Carlton Cinema on its final day before closing, October 29, 1977.

Good Sports

A scramble in the girls' obstacle race at the youth athletics tournament, held at St Helen's sports ground, July 27, 1950.

Swansea N S F Ladies Football Club with officials, 1918.

Hafod Boys School soccer team, 1950-1951. The teachers, from left are messrs Morris and Eustace.

South Wales Transport employees' Magnet Club Cricket X1 after playing opponents from the Midland Red bus company at Worcester's county ground at Dudley, 1952.

Dynevor Grammar School's cricket XI in July 1953 after their annual match with the old Dyvorians at St. Helen's in which they were defeated.

An aerial view of the last
Welsh rugby international to
be played at St Helen's
sports ground,
March 22, 1952.

The shinty team at Powys Avenue Mixed Junior School, 1962. Shinty is a junior form of hockey.

Members of Swansea Wayfarers Cycling Club pictured during a run to the top of the Neath Valley, 1958.

An Evening Post women's football team, 1963.

A National Coal Board football team 1964. The NCB offices were all in the Cambrian Place area including Exchange Buildings, Cambrian House, Pembroke Buildings, Atlantic House and Gloucester Chambers. In 1965 all of these premises were vacated and staff transferred to Tondu, Bridgend.

Competitors battle it out in an autocross event at Fairwood, Gower on May 10, 1964. The class was for sports cars up to 1100 cc and car number 40 came first in its class.

Clwyd Junior School rugby team at St Helen's Ground in 1972 after a cup final which ended with the drawn result Clwyd 4 - Dunvant 4.

Participants in a bowls match at the 'Tick Tock' clock and watch factory at Ystradgynlais, September 1973.

Glamorgan County Cricketer Jim Presdee arrives in style at his benefit match at St Helen's, 1964.